BOOK &
DVD
IDEO

BLUES HARMONICA

Authentic Styles & Techniques of the Great Harp Players

★★★★★ BY ★★★★★

STEVE GUYGER

Edited by Chad Johnson

ISBN 978-1-4584-1969-9

HAL•LEONARD®
CORPORATION
7777 W. BLUEMOUND RD. P.O. BOX 13819 MILWAUKEE, WI 53213

In Australia Contact:
Hal Leonard Australia Pty. Ltd.
4 Lentara Court
Cheltenham, Victoria, 3192 Australia
Email: ausadmin@halleonard.com.au

Visit Hal Leonard Online at
www.halleonard.com

TABLE OF CONTENTS

INTRODUCTION

The harmonica is tightly woven into the history of American blues music. Its distinctive wail has graced countless classic recordings dating back to the early 20th century up through the present, and it shows no signs of losing favor anytime soon. It's hard to imagine those early Muddy Waters records without the harp contributions by the great Little Walter, and Howlin' Wolf's "Smokestack Lightning" wouldn't be the same without his brief but poignant harp breaks that answer his falsetto howls. Simply put, Chicago blues wouldn't be Chicago blues without the harmonica.

In this book/DVD package, I'll share the insights and concepts that have served me well in my 40 years plus of playing the harmonica. After being inspired originally by Paul Butterfield in the late '60s, I made several trips to Chicago to learn blues harp at the feet of the masters. With each trip, I learned more valuable lessons that I took back with me to my home in Philadelphia and incorporated into what would become my own style.

Over the years, I've had the good fortune to play with many legends along the way, including Jimmy Rogers, Hubert Sumlin, Sunnyland Slim, Eddie Taylor, Big Guitar Red, and Louisiana Red. In addition, I've also fronted my own band, the Excellos, for over 30 years. It's now my goal to share my knowledge and experience with you in the hopes of furthering your understanding of blues harp. I hope you enjoy the journey.

-Steve Guyger

ABOUT THE DVD

The DVD that accompanies this book contains performances of many concepts and ideas presented here. Each time a demonstration appears on the DVD, you'll see an icon  to let you know. However, you should certainly view the DVD in its entirety at some point, because it contains additional concepts and demonstrations of its own that are valuable to the fledgling blues harp player.

HISTORY OF THE HARMONICA

Predecessors of the modern harmonica date back to the early 19th century, when a German named Christian Buschmann created a 4" x 4" square-shaped collection of 15 pitch pipes and called it the Buschmann Aura (circa 1820). The instrument could only be blown and was extremely limited by today's standards, but it became fairly popular in Germany and Austria at the time. A giant leap forward appeared shortly after in the form of the "Vamper." This was an instrument designed by an immigrant from Bohemia known only by his last name: Richter. Remarkably similar to the modern day harp, it contained a 10-hole diatonic layout and could produce notes by blowing and drawing. The instrument was viewed with great skepticism and curiosity, and never really caught on.

However, the widespread popularity of the modern-day harmonica is attributable almost entirely to one man: a German named Mathias Hohner. Since the 1850s, Hohner, a clockmaker by trade, had been building "mouth organs" in his spare time. Around 1865, he shipped a supply of these to America with the hopes that his cousins (recent American immigrants) could establish a market for them. The superior tone, quality construction, and portability of the Hohner harmonica quickly established the instrument in the States, and its popularity spread rapidly.

Fast forward nearly 100 years, and you start to hear the term "Chicago Blues." This was a time when the harmonica was out in front of the band, taking most of the solos. As the great blues pianist Otis Spann put it, "The harmonica was the mother of the band." Most of the players we'll discuss in this book actually weren't from Chicago. Many were from different areas of the Deep South—including Memphis, Tennessee and the Mississippi Delta—and eventually migrated to Chicago to join the blossoming blues scene spearheaded by the likes of Muddy Waters and John Lee Hooker.

Photo courtesy of Joel Whitburn

Muddy Waters

Many harp players knew each other long before they came to Chicago. Some of these early blues harp pioneers on record include Jaybird Coleman, Jazz Gillum, Hammie Nixon, and the most popular harp player of all: John Lee "Sonny Boy" Williamson (a.k.a. Sonny Boy I). Williamson began recording in 1937 with his first song, "Good Morning Little Schoolgirl" and lived in Chicago until his untimely death in 1948. The shadow he cast on the blues harp world is as great as any.

Little Walter Jacobs

John Lee "Sonny Boy" Williamson

The mid to late '40s brought a new crop of blues harp players, and most were largely influenced by Sonny Boy I. Some of the most popular included Snooky Pryor, Big Walter Horton, Forest City Joe, and Little Walter Jacobs—the latter considered by many to be the greatest blues harp player of them all. Though he made his name playing with Muddy Waters in 1952, it was the release of his first solo record, *Juke* (Chess Records), that made everyone in the country want to play the harmonica.

The '50s brought with it many more great players, including Howlin' Wolf, Jimmy Reed, Junior Wells, George Smith, James Cotton, and Alex William Miller (Rice Miller), who was also known as "Sonny Boy Williamson"—an ongoing problem for blues historians. A unique player with his own style, Rice Miller has since been designated by many as Sonny Boy II in an effort to clear up the confusion.

HARMONICA BASICS

Though harmonicas come in various types and sizes, we'll focus mostly on one type in this book: the **diatonic harmonica**. It's by far the most commonly used and therefore makes a great place to start. We'll also briefly look at another common type: the **chromatic harmonica**, or **chromonica**.

THE DIATONIC (10-HOLE) HARMONICA

The diatonic, or 10-hole harmonica, is the most common harmonica of all and is what most people think of when they hear the word. It's a small instrument that consists of three basic parts: the **comb**, **reed plates**, and **cover plates**.

The comb is basically the body of the instrument. Originally made of wood, it is usually made of plastic or metal these days. The comb channels the air's flow through the instrument and houses the reed plates, which are usually made of brass. These are bolted or screwed to the comb and contain the attached reeds that vibrate when air is blown or sucked through the harmonica. The cover plates cover the reed plates; they're what you hold onto as you play. Usually made from metal, they also come in wood and plastic occasionally.

Where Does the "Diatonic" Name Come From?

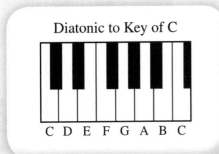

The word "diatonic" basically means "belonging to one key." It refers to a scale or piece of music in which all the notes belong to the same key. For example, in the key of C, which contains no sharps or flats, the notes C, D, E, F, G, A, and B are diatonic.

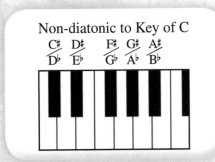

That's seven different notes—all the white keys on the piano. There are twelve notes altogether though, so any of the other five notes would require a sharp or flat and would be considered "non-diatonic" to the key of C.

A diatonic harmonica, or "harp," is designed to play in only one key and contains only the notes of that key's **major scale**. (See "Chord Theory Primer" in Appendix for more on major scales.) If you want to play in the key of C major, you'd use a C harmonica. To play in G major, you'd use a G harp, etc. Therefore, you can find diatonic harmonicas in all twelve major keys.

In practical application, however—especially blues playing—this is a bit misleading, because we can actually play in more than one key on a diatonic harp. In fact, in blues harp playing, it's actually more common to play in a different key than that of the harp! We'll talk more about this in later chapters.

The 10-Hole Note Layout

Let's look at the basic layout of the 10-hole harp. You'll notice that the numbers are engraved or printed above the holes along the top of the harmonica, progressing left to right from lowest to highest. The pitches of the harmonica also progress low to high from left to right, just like a piano. We'll use a C harp for demonstration purposes, but all diatonic harps will follow this basic layout with regard to the scale degrees.

Blow Notes: C-Tuned Harmonica

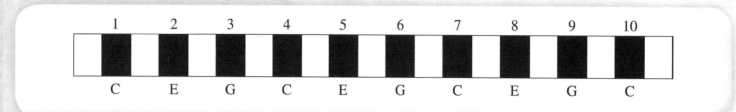

As you can see, the blow notes consist of only three different pitches: C, E, and G. These pitches create a C **major chord**, which is the **tonic** chord in the key of C. We can play C chords in several different **octaves** by blowing.

Draw (Inhaled) Notes: C-Tuned Harmonica

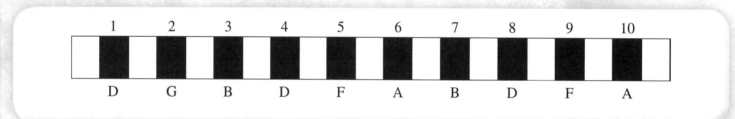

By drawing, we have access to the other four notes in the key of C: D, B, F, and A. Notice that the note G is available as a blow *and* draw note. We're also able to play a few other chords—most notably a G chord (G–B–D), which is the **V chord** in the key of C, and a Dm chord (D–F–A), which is the **ii chord**.

THE CHROMATIC HARMONICA (CHROMONICA)

The **chromatic harmonica**, or "chromonica," can most easily be described as two harmonicas a half step apart (a C harmonica and a C♯/D♭ harmonica, for example) stacked on top of each other in one casing. By pressing a button, a sliding bar covers up the holes of one, leaving the other open. Therefore, you switch between the two harmonicas by pressing or releasing the button. They're a good bit larger than a standard 10-hole diatonic harmonica.

Chromatic harmonicas are actually available in all twelve keys, but most players use a C chromatic (which is paired with a C♯/D♭), perhaps because it's the most familiar, and you have access to all the notes anyway (as you do with a chromatic harp in any key). Chromonicas are not extremely common in blues, although there are recorded examples of Little Walter and others. One of the reasons is that the tuning system (note layout) is different. In a chromatic harmonica, the note layout is usually the same in each octave (known as "solo tuning") as opposed to the layout of the diatonic (known as "Richter tuning").

12-hole chromatic and 10-hole diatonic harmonicas

Standard C Chromatic Harmonica Note Layout

Blow Notes

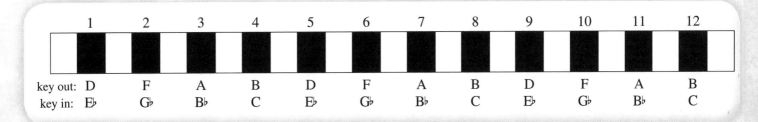

	1	2	3	4	5	6	7	8	9	10	11	12
key out:	C	E	G	C	C	E	G	C	C	E	G	C
key in:	D♭	F	A♭	D♭	D♭	F	A♭	D♭	D♭	F	A♭	D♭

Draw Notes

	1	2	3	4	5	6	7	8	9	10	11	12
key out:	D	F	A	B	D	F	A	B	D	F	A	B
key in:	E♭	G♭	B♭	C	E♭	G♭	B♭	C	E♭	G♭	B♭	C

Among other things, this means that the chords available on a chromatic harmonica are not that of a diatonic, making it more suitable for lead melodies. It's also nearly impossible to **overblow** (we'll touch on this later) on a chromatic harmonica, except on the last four holes.

Because of these differences, chromatic harps are favored more by jazz and classical players, though some pop musicians have made use of them too—most notably Stevie Wonder and John Lennon. That's pretty much it for our discussion of the chromatic. From now on, we'll focus our studies strictly on the diatonic 10-hole.

HOLDING THE HARP

Let's get started by learning how to hold the harmonica. Almost all harmonica players hold the harp in their left hand. (This may seem counterintuitive to a right-handed person, but realize that the right hand does come into play for techniques such as wah-wah, fanning, and trilling, all of which we'll look at later on.) Begin by gripping it with the thumb and first finger. The numbers should be right-side up, and there should be enough area exposed in front of your thumb and finger so that you can place your mouth on it.

There are those who play with the bass notes on the right side (the numbers upside down), and if you've already started that way and feel comfortable with it, feel free to continue. All references in this book to hole numbers, however, will be from the right-side up perspective.

PRODUCING NOTES

There are three different methods commonly used to produce notes on the harmonica. Let's take a brief look at each.

Pressing Your Lips

This is the easiest and most basic method used to play notes on the harmonica. You simply press your lips to a hole and blow or draw (suck) air through it. Try to center your lips on the hole and close around it tightly enough so that only one note is produced. Of course, you can (and will) blow through more than one hole to generate **chords** (several notes played simultaneously), but it's critical to be able to play one note at a time, especially in blues soloing.

Practice first blowing each of the ten holes, from lowest to highest, aiming for a clean, single tone throughout. When you get to the top, try drawing on each hole, from high to low, again striving for one note each time. Do this several times until it begins to feel natural.

Tongue Blocking

With the tongue blocking method, you press your tongue against several holes and cover more of the harmonica with your mouth. There should be enough space to the right (usually) of your tongue to allow one note to sound.

Obviously, this method is not used as much on the lower notes, as there are no holes for you to block when playing through hole 1. Still, try working through the full range of the harmonica, blowing up through the holes and drawing down through them as before, to get the feel for this technique.

Curled Tongue

The last method we'll examine is the curled tongue. With this technique, you curl your tongue into a little tunnel shape and blow or draw through it. This technique takes some getting used to, so you may have to work at it.

Again, try blowing and drawing your way up and down through the holes one at a time to get used to this.

You'll notice that each method has a distinct sound. With experience, you'll learn how to make use of each to help express yourself on the harp. I encourage you to try mastering each one, as they're all useful sounds.

C MAJOR SCALE

Although we have access to 20 notes on a 10-hole diatonic harp, we actually only have one full major scale. Let's learn how to play a C major scale on a C harp. The notes of the C major scale are C–D–E–F–G–A–B. It's the only major scale that uses no sharped (♯) or flatted (♭) notes. We'll be using holes 4 through 7 to play it.

4th hole blow = C

4th hole draw = D

5th hole blow = E

5th hole draw = F

6th hole blow = G

6th hole draw = A

7th hole draw = B

7th hole blow = C

Notice that the pattern of blow/draw/blow/draw changes for hole 7, so keep an eye (or ear) out for that. You also need to be especially careful when drawing on hole 6 to make sure you're only sounding one note. If you accidentally draw in on hole 7 as well, you'll get the A and B notes together, which doesn't usually sound all that pretty.

Try running up and down the scale a few times, concentrating on getting a good, clear sound out of each note. When moving from draw 7 to draw 6, you don't need to stop the inhale. You can just smoothly slide from hole to hole for a connected sound.

The "Breathing Note"

If you look back at page 8, you'll notice that draw 2 and blow 3 are the same note: G (on a C harp). This is referred to as a "breathing note" because it allows you to play the same note with a blow and a draw. This aids in phrasing by providing you with a choice of where you want to play that note. Try moving between these two notes to get a feel for this; try to make the transition as seamless as possible.

BASS NOTE CHORDS IN C

Let's now quickly look at two bass-note chords in C that you'll find very useful when accompanying yourself or others.

C Major Chord (I)

The first is the **I chord** (read "the one chord") of the key. In the key of C major, this is a C major chord. It's called the I chord because it's built from the first note of the major scale. The notes of a C chord are C, E, and G, and so we can play it by blowing on holes 1, 2, and 3.

1st hole blow = C

2nd hole blow = E

3rd hole blow = G

Try it now. As opposed to playing single notes, when playing chords you'll need to cover much more of the harp with your mouth to allow three holes to sound at once.

G Major Chord (V)

The second chord we'll learn is the V chord in the key of C. This is a G major chord, and it contains the notes G, B, and D. Again, it's called the V chord because it's built off the fifth note of the C major scale: C (1)–D (2)–E (3)–F (4)–**G (5)**. We'll play this chord by drawing on holes 1, 2, and 3.

1st hole draw = D

2nd hole draw = G

3rd hole draw = B

Notice that the notes of this chord aren't in order the way the notes of the C chord were. In other words, in the C chord, the C note, or **root**, was in the bottom. In this G chord, the D note is in the bottom. That's ok. As long as the three different notes of the chord (G, B, and D) are present, it'll still sound like a V chord.

HARMONICA NOTATION TUTORIAL

Harmonica music is normally written in one of two ways: with standard musical notation, or with the number/arrow system. These aren't entirely exclusive, because standard notation for the harmonica is often supplemented with the number/arrow system. Let's look briefly at each method. Since the number/arrow system is the easiest to learn, we'll start there.

NUMBER/ARROW NOTATION

This is sometimes called **harmonica tablature** (or "tab" for short), and it can't really be more simplified. There are two elements: a number and an arrow. The number tells you which hole to play, and the arrow tells you whether to blow or draw. An arrow pointing up indicates a blow, and one pointing down indicates a draw.

4↑   5↑   5↓   6↑

The example above tells you to:
Blow 4
Blow 5
Draw 5
Blow 6

You may also see the arrow beneath the number as a variation:

4   5   5   6
↑   ↑   ↓   ↑

Couldn't be simpler, right? This is an excellent method to use when notating a song that almost everyone knows, such as "Amazing Grace" or "Twinkle, Twinkle Little Star." For example, here's how the first phrase of "Twinkle, Twinkle Little Star" would appear using the number/arrow system.

4↑   4↑   6↑   6↑   6↓   6↓   6↑
Twin - kle,   twin - kle   lit - tle   star,

5↓   5↓   5↑   5↑   4↓   4↓   4↑
How   I   won - der   what   you   are.

But this system has a major drawback in that it doesn't tell you the **rhythm** of the notes. In other words, it doesn't tell you how long or short to play each note. As mentioned, if you're familiar with the tune, this isn't a big deal. You can even write lyrics beneath the numbers (as shown above) to make it really clear. But if you're reading music to a song you don't know, you're left in the dark. This is where standard notation comes into play.

STANDARD NOTATION

The Staff

Standard notation conveys two different things: **pitch** and **rhythm**. Music notation is written on a set of five lines called a **staff**. Notes are written on either the **lines** or the **spaces** in between the lines.

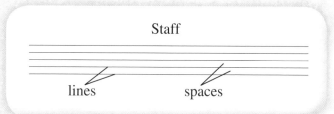

A **clef** tells you what notes are assigned to the lines and spaces. Harmonica music is written on a **treble clef**, which is the most common type of clef. When the staff uses this type of clef, the notes on the lines, from low to high, are E, G, B, D, and F. The spaces, from low to high, are F, A, C, and E. Many people remember the lines by making up phrases such as "**E**very **G**ood **B**oy **D**oes **F**ine." The spaces are really easy to remember because they spell "FACE."

Note that, taken together, the ascending lines and spaces progress straight through the musical alphabet, which makes use of the letters A–G.

Pitch

The pitch (highness or lowness of a note) is shown vertically. Notes higher on the staff are higher pitched than those lower on the staff.

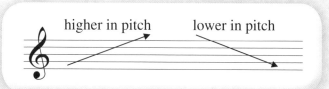

Ledger Lines

When notes move higher or lower than the lines of the staff, temporary **ledger lines** are drawn in to accommodate. The pitches continue through the musical alphabet in the same way.

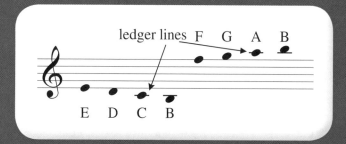

Rhythm

Different types of notes indicate the rhythm, or how long the notes are held. Each rhythmic note value also has a corresponding **rest**, which indicates silence (i.e., you play nothing). Note that the whole note is the only note that does not have a **stem**.

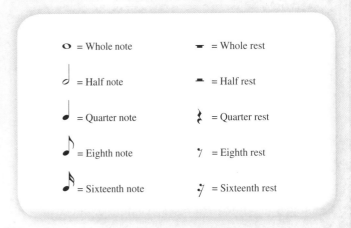

From this chart, we can see that:
- One whole note = two half notes
- One half note = two quarter notes
- One quarter note = two eighth notes
- One eighth note = two sixteenth notes

Measures

We count the rhythm of music using **beats**. On the staff, **bar lines** divide the music into **measures** (or **bars**), which are smaller groups of beats.

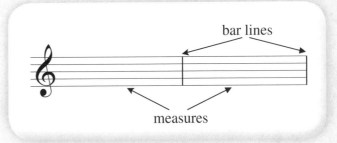

Think of measures like sentences and bar lines like periods. A book would be pretty difficult to read if there were no periods to break up the sentences. Similarly, it would be easy to lose your spot in music if it weren't broken up into measures.

Time Signature

The **time signature** appears on the staff at the very beginning of a piece of music. It consists of two numbers. The top number tells you how many beats are in each measure, and the bottom number tells you which rhythmic value is considered a beat.

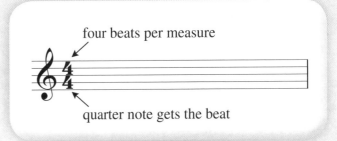

The most common time signature is **4/4** (also known as **common time**), which tells us that there are four beats in a measure and the quarter note (1/4) is counted as one beat.

A time signature of **3/4** would tell us that there are three beats in a measure, and the quarter note gets the beat. Other common time signatures include **12/8** (twelve beats in a measure, and the eighth note gets the beat) and **6/8** (six beats in a measure, and the eighth note gets the beat).

COMBINING THE TWO SYSTEMS

In this book, we'll combine the two systems for the most clarity. Here's how our "Twinkle, Twinkle Little Star" melody from earlier would look with this method.

This way, even if you're not familiar with the rhythm of the melody, you can read it in the notation. Other elements of standard notation and harmonica tab exist as well, and we'll cover those as they arise later in the book.

TIPS ON SOUND AND TONE

Once you start getting comfortable with producing notes on the harmonica, you can start to think about the difference between **sound** and **tone**. The sound is inherent in the instrument, whereas the tone is something you create. Without tone, the instrument can sound bland and lack depth.

CREATING TONE

Everyone has their own tone, and this makes each player sound different. It would be quite a dull world if everyone sounded the same. There are certain aspects of your tone that you're born with. This has to do with things like the size of your mouth, shape of your lips, etc. But within those parameters, there's a huge amount of variation available. Listen to the DVD for a demonstration between the difference of the natural sound of the harmonica and the tone I create.

What I'm doing to create the different tones is channeling the air a bit differently instead of letting it all naturally flow through the harp. This is something that you can experiment with until you find a tone (or tones) that you like. Among other things, the tone can be affected by:

* The shape of your lips against the hole
* The placement of your tongue inside your mouth
* The angle of the harmonica against your mouth
* The amount of the harmonica you cover with your mouth (you can cover more surface area of the harp but still only allow one note to sound)
* The placement of your hands around the harp (we'll talk more about this later)

By experimenting with the above concepts, you can create bright, dark, intense, mellow, clear, or muffled tones and anything in between. Listen to recordings of your favorite harmonica players and try to duplicate what you hear. Chances are you won't be able to exactly replicate someone else's tone, but in the process, you'll likely develop a tone that's unique to you.

Little Walter Jacobs

Photo courtesy of Joel Whitburn

John Lee "Sonny Boy" Williamson (a.k.a "Sonny Boy I")

BREATHING

Another important aspect of tone production is breathing. It's perhaps extra critical in harmonica playing because we produce notes by both exhaling and inhaling—something that's unique about the harp.

From the Diaphragm

When playing harmonica, you should try to breathe from the diaphragm. This is the same thing that most singers and wind players do, and the reason is that you'll get better air control, which will result in a more powerful and stable tone. Just as a glass gets filled up with water from the bottom, so should your lungs fill with air.

Try lying on your back and breathing in (drawing) through the harmonica. Visualize filling your lungs up with air from the bottom until they're completely full. Then exhale through the harp and hold the note for as long as possible. When you think you've run out of air, exhale a bit more. Repeat this process over and over until you're able to produce clear, steady tones on both the draw and the blow.

Your stomach should be moving in and out while playing as the diaphragm expands and contracts. Watch the DVD to see how this happens as I play.

Try playing the following exercises on a C harp, and concentrate on a steady, solid tone throughout. You may have to play at a faster tempo at first if you're having trouble holding out the notes.

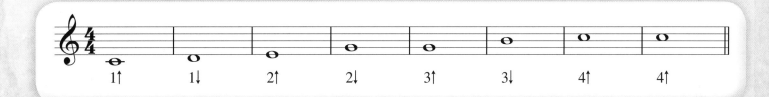

(Note: The *8va* symbol means that you should play an octave higher than written; the *loco* symbol means to revert back to written pitch.)

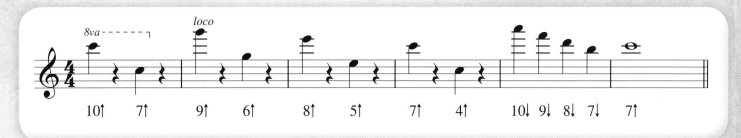

CHORDS AND CHORD PROGRESSIONS

Let's look a bit more at some different chords we can play. We'll be using a C harp here.

G CHORDS

On the C harp, G is a common chord. It's the V chord in the key of C, and it's the I chord when we use the C harp to play in the key of G, which is called playing **cross harp**. (We'll talk more about this later.)

Let's begin with a two-note chord, G–B, which we play by drawing on holes 2 and 3.

Here's a three-note chord, G–B–D, which we'll play by drawing on holes 2, 3, and 4.

And here's a G chord drawing on the first four holes: D–G–B–D.

In this next chord, we're playing a G7 fragment: D–G–F. We do this by drawing on holes 1–5 and using our tongue to block holes 3 and 4. So the only notes we should be hearing are draw 1 (D), draw 2 (G), and draw 5 (F). This tongue blocking technique will take some getting used to, so don't get discouraged if you're not able to do it right away. Experiment with the placement of your mouth, lips, and tongue, and you'll eventually get it.

C CHORDS

Now let's look at some C chords on the C harp. This would be the I chord when playing in the key of C or the IV chord when playing cross harp in the key of G.

For this first one, we'll blow on holes 1–4 to get C–E–G–C.

Here's a nice sounding one blowing on holes 3, 4, and 5 to get G–C–E.

Now let's blow on holes 2, 3, and 4 to get E–G–C.

And finally, here's a higher, two-note version that we play by blowing on holes 5 and 6 to get E–G. Even though there's no C (root) in this chord, it'll still sound like a C chord if we're playing in the key of C or G.

F CHORD

The last C chord fragment we played is nice for alternating with this two-note F chord of F–A. We play it by drawing on holes 5 and 6. An F chord is the IV chord in the key of C, and it would be the ♭VII chord in the key of G.

OCTAVES

Though not technically chords, playing octaves on the harp is similar to playing chords, so we're covering it here. An octave is simply the same note in two different registers. In other words, if we played only the top and bottom notes of our C major scale (**C**–D–E–F–G–A–B–**C**), we would be playing octave C notes.

The first octave shape we'll look at is on holes 1 and 4. Using your tongue to block holes 2 and 3, blow and draw holes 1 and 4 to get C and D octaves, respectively. Again, as with the G7 chord, this'll take some experimenting.

Here are some other octaves that you can play on the harmonica as well. Blowing holes 2 and 5 (and blocking holes 3 and 4) will give you octave E notes.

Blowing on holes 5 and 8 will give you octave E notes. (Note that you can't draw on these holes to get an octave, because draw 5 is an F note, and draw 8 is a D.)

Blowing on holes 3 and 6 (and blocking holes 4 and 5) will give you octave G notes. (Note that you can't draw on these holes to get an octave, because draw 3 is a B note, and draw 6 is an A.)

Blowing on holes 6 and 9 will give you octave G notes. (Note that you can't draw on these holes to get an octave, because draw 6 is an A note, and draw 9 is an F.)

Blowing on holes 4 and 7 will give you octave C notes. (Note that you can't draw on these holes to get an octave, because draw 4 is a D note, and draw 7 is a B.)

Blowing on holes 7 and 10 will give you octave C notes. (Note that you can't draw on these holes to get an octave, because draw 7 is a B note, and draw 10 is an A.)

There are other possibilities for octaves on draw notes, but they're much more difficult because the holes are four spaces apart instead of three, as with the blow octaves. Draw holes 3 and 7, 4 and 8, 5 and 9, and 6 and 10 (with holes blocked in between) will give you octave B, D, F, and A notes, respectively.

THE I–IV–V CHORDS

In a blues song, we almost always use three chords of the key: the I, IV, and V. As long as you know a key's major scale, you'll know what the I, IV, and V chords are. You just simply count the notes of the scale until you find the first (root or **tonic**), fourth (known as the **subdominant**), and fifth (known as the **dominant**) notes of the scale. You can quickly find all twelve major scales spelled out for you online if necessary.

So, for example, in the key of C, the I, IV, and V chords would be C, F, and G.

C	D	E	F	G	A	B
1	2	3	**4**	**5**	6	7
I			**IV**	**V**		

(When counting degrees of a scale, we normally use numbers, but when talking about chords, we normally use Roman numerals.)

In the key of G, the I, IV, and V chords would be G, C, and D.

G	A	B	C	D	E	F♯
1	2	3	**4**	**5**	6	7
I			**IV**	**V**		

In the key of A, the I, IV, and V chords would be A, D, and E.

A	B	C♯	D	E	F♯	G♯
1	2	3	**4**	**5**	6	7
I			**IV**	**V**		

And so on. I'd advise you to take some time and get familiar with this progression in all twelve keys. Although certain keys are more common when playing blues with a guitar player (such as E and A), different ones are more common when playing with horn players (such as B♭ and E♭).

Ties and Key Signatures

In music, a **tie** simply joins the rhythmic values of two notes together as one. So if a quarter note (one beat) is tied to a half note (two beats), you'd hold the note for three beats. Ties can appear within a measure or across bar lines.

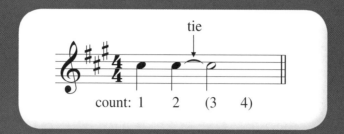

Also notice the collection of sharp (♯) signs at the beginning immediately following the treble clef. This is called a **key signature**, and it tells the performer that every time they see those notes (F, C, and G), they should play their sharp versions (F♯, C♯, and G♯, respectively) instead. This helps avoid having to write out the same sharps (or flats) over and over, and it also lets the performer know that the song is in the key of A—i.e., A is the tonic note. So, the notes above are actually C♯ notes, not C notes.

Keep an eye out for both the key signature and the ties in this next example.

If you have an A harp, try playing along with this riff from the DVD. On the DVD, I'm just playing root notes of the I, IV, and V chords; you can play the chords notated, and it will sound great. Eventually, you can play the root notes the way I am, but I'm using the bending technique to play the root of the IV chord (D), which is a bit more advanced. We'll look at that a bit later.

Here are the chords you'll be using. Practice these individually before trying to play the riff.

I chord (A):   4↑ 5↑ 6↑

IV chord (D): 5↓ 6↓

V chord (E): 2↓ 3↓ 4↓

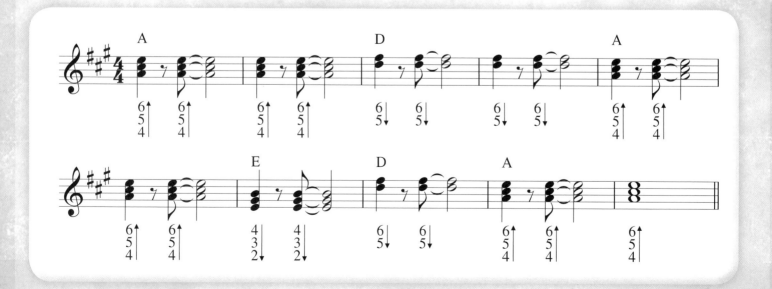

12-BAR BLUES FORM

The vast majority of blues songs use the same chord progression with only minor variation. This progression lasts for twelve measures and is known as the **12-bar blues**. The basic form looks like this:

- Four measures on I
- Two measures on IV
- Two measures on I
- One measure on V
- One measure on IV
- Two measures on I

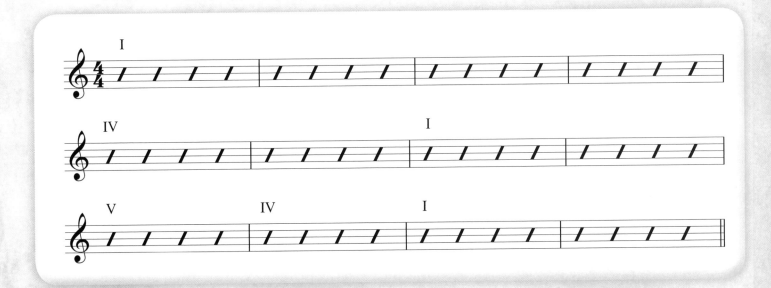

In the key of A, it would look like this:

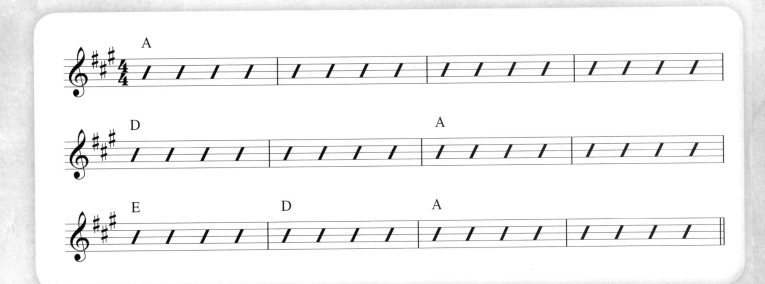

There are a lot of variations on this, but this is the basic idea. You've probably heard this progression in thousands of songs over the years, as it's extremely common in rock, pop, jazz, and country, as well as blues.

Check out the DVD to hear me playing over a 12-bar progression in the key of E with a guitar accompaniment provided by my good friend, Billy Flynn. Here are the chords in the key of E:

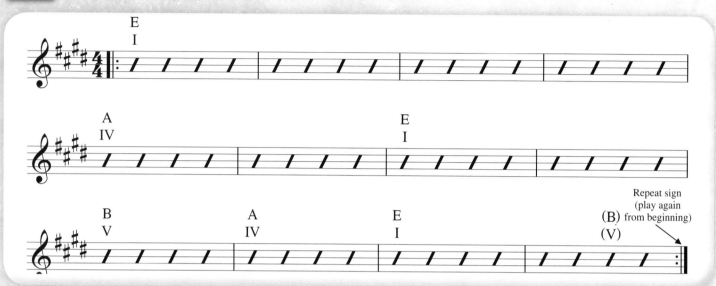

A really common variation on this is called a **quick change**. In a quick change, we move to the IV chord in measure 2 and back to the I chord for measures 3 and 4. Everything else is the same. You can hear me demonstrate this on the DVD at the end of the Playing Chords section.

8-BAR BLUES FORM

Another common blues form is the **8-bar blues**. Its chord structure is different from the 12-bar, and there are some variations on it as well. One common form looks like this:

- Two measures on I
- Two measures on IV
- One measure on I
- One measure on V
- Two measures on I

Here's what it sounds like with me playing over an 8-bar blues in E.

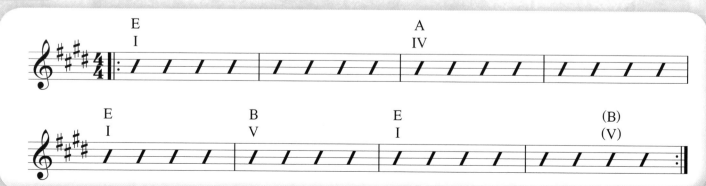

I-CHORD BLUES

Another form of the blues is the **I-chord blues**. This simply remains on the I chord throughout, and the players often take turns riffing off it. Here's what it sounds like with me playing over a I-chord blues in E.

INTERMEDIATE AND ADVANCED TECHNIQUES

Now that you've gotten used to producing notes and chords on the harp, let's examine a few more techniques that help lend a blues flavor to your playing. Though each one of these techniques is useful, don't feel the need to *always* use them; the possible exception to this is bending, which you will use constantly when playing blues harp. These techniques provide unique colors and effects and can start to sound novel if used extensively.

BENDING

One of the most important techniques in all of blues harp playing is bending. It simply wouldn't sound bluesy if you weren't able to bend on a harp—not to mention the fact that you don't even have access to certain notes without bending down to them. When we bend, the notes always bend down to a lower pitch. Because of the way the harp is set up, we can only bend draw notes on holes 1–6 and blow notes on holes 7–10. It's usually easier to master bends on the lower (draw) holes, so let's start there.

Draw Bends

Try drawing on hole 2 and listen to the pitch. On a C harp, this will be a G note. Now, try drawing again but try any or all of the following until you start to hear the note drop in pitch down to F:

- Constrict the air flow in your throat
- Drop your jaw
- Move your tongue around
- Say "ooh" silently while drawing
- Tense your lips and/or cover more of the harp with your mouth
- Draw in the air with more force than normal

Bending takes practice and experimentation, but hopefully one of those above suggestions made something happen to the note. Eventually, it'll click, and you'll "get it." Because of the changes you have to make to your mouth and lips in order to create the bend, a bent note will sound different than a regular draw note. This is normal, and it only adds to the expressiveness of the harp. Not every hole can be bent the same amount of pitch. Here's how draw bends work:

- Holes 1, 4, 5, and 6 can only be bent down a half step.
- Hole 2 can be bent down a whole step.
- Hole 3 can be bent down 1 1/2 steps (a whole step plus a half step).

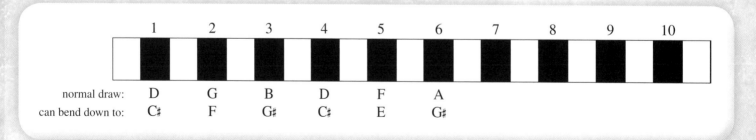

	1	2	3	4	5	6	7	8	9	10
normal draw:	D	G	B	D	F	A				
can bend down to:	C♯	F	G♯	C♯	E	G♯				

It's important to note that you can bend down to any in-between pitch as well. For example, if you can bend down a whole step (as on draw 2), you can also bend down a half step. If you can bend down 1 1/2 steps (as on draw 3), you can also bend down a half step and a whole step.

A **half step** is the smallest distance between any two notes. It's the distance of a white piano key to the black key adjacent to it or the distance of one fret on a guitar. For example, from C to C♯ is a half step. A **whole step** is twice that of a half step. For example, from C to D is a whole step.

In the tab, we'll use the following symbols to indicate bends:

⤵ = half step bend
⤵ = whole step bend
⤵ = 1½ step bend (rare)

Shuffle Feel

Most blues is played with what's known as a **shuffle feel**. This means that the eighth notes are uneven—the first in each beat lasting longer than the second. Think of a song like "Pride and Joy" or "I'm Tore Down," and you're hearing a shuffle feel. It's something you'll immediately recognize when you hear it, and you've definitely heard it hundreds of times. The song we play on the intro to the accompanying DVD is played as a quick shuffle.

You can also think about it from a technical standpoint. If you divide the beat into three equal parts instead of two, you have what's known as a **triplet**. You can count triplets as "one-and-uh, two-and-uh, three-and-uh, four-and-uh," etc. When playing eighth notes in a shuffle feel, the first eighth note will last as long as the first two parts of the triplet, and the second will last only as long as the last part of the triplet. In sheet music, to indicate that a song is to be played with this feel, either the terms "shuffle feel" or "swing feel" will usually appear at the beginning. Alternatively, you may see this symbol, which means the same thing:

$$\left(\sqcap\!\sqcap = \overset{3}{\sqcap} \right)$$

Draw Bend Practice Licks

Try this phrase with a C harp; notice the shuffle feel indication in the music. Play it nice and slow so you can really concentrate on getting the feel for the bend. We're bending the drawn G note on hole 2 down a whole step to F. To make sure you're getting the bent F note in tune, check its pitch against the F on the fifth hole draw note. This F note will be an octave higher than the one you're bending on draw 2, but the *pitches* should still sound the same (one will be a higher F, and one will be a lower F).

Let's try another bend on a C harp. This time, we'll be bending the draw note on hole 3 (B) down a half step to B♭. This one may be a bit tougher than the first, because it's "in the cracks," meaning that it's not the farthest note you can bend down to. Be aware that this is a **pre-bend**, meaning that the unbent note (B) should not be heard at all; the B♭ should be produced immediately. Since we don't have a naturally occurring B♭ note on the C harp, find another instrument to play a B♭ note on so you can check your pitch. A keyboard would be ideal because you can play the keys with one hand while holding the harp with the other.

Blow Bends

On holes 7, 8, 9, and 10, we create bends by blowing instead of drawing. These are a bit more difficult for most people to master, and, consequently, they're not used as often as draw bends. They do, however, open up a lot of possibilities for melodic ideas, so I encourage you to learn them. Jimmy Reed is someone to check out if you'd like to hear mastery of blow bends.

Incidentally, blow bends are easier in lower-keyed harps like G and A. They're very difficult, if not impossible, on an F harp, for example. So you may want to try to learn the technique on a G or A harp if you have one. I'll demonstrate them with a C harp here.

Start with hole 9 and blow lightly. You should hear a pure G note. Now try pursing your lips a bit more and raising your tongue. You may need to blow a little harder as well. Play around with these ideas until you start to hear a dip in pitch to F♯. Again, as with draw bends, it takes experimentation. You'll eventually find it.

As with the draw bends, not every hole can be bent the same amount of pitch. Here's how the blow bends work:

- Hole 7 can only be bent down one half step.
- Holes 8, 9, and 10 can be bent down a whole step.

= half step blow bend
= whole step blow bend

	1	2	3	4	5	6	7	8	9	10
normal draw:							C	E	G	C
can bend down to:							B	D	F	B♭

Blow Bend Practice Licks

Try this lick on a C harp to work on your blow bends. We're performing two half-step bends here: the ninth hole blow from G down to F♯ and the eighth hole blow from E down to E♭. Again, check your pitches on a keyboard if possible.

Here's another phrase where we're bending the E on hole 8 down a half step to E♭. Start slowly at first and check the pitch of the bent note. Notice the first group of notes are an **eighth-note triplet**, meaning three notes are played in that beat instead of two.

Using Bends to Play a Low Major Scale

Earlier in the book, we learned a C major scale on the diatonic C harp by playing holes 4–7. By using bends, we can also play a major scale from holes 1–4. To do this, we'll use two draw bends: one on hole 2 and one on hole 3. Try this slowly at first and then try playing along with the DVD.

WAH-WAH

Your hands can be very effective tools when expressing yourself on the harmonica. One of the most common effects created is the **wah-wah**. Let's start with a slow wah. Try drawing on hole 2 with your C harp. Cup your right hand (as if holding water) around the front of the harp and, while drawing the note, pull your hand away and return it to the cupped position. You should hear the note go from dark to bright and back to dark.

You can also create a faster wah by cupping your hand in the same way. Instead of moving your entire hand away though, you simply flutter your fingers to create a smaller opening. Try it on the same draw 2 note with your C harp.

Many harmonica players, such as Big Walter Horton or "Sonny Boy II" (Rice Miller), keep their right-hand thumb behind the harp (on the side with the holes) when performing the wah technique. I don't do that because my hands are smaller than most players, and I can't create a large enough air chamber with my thumb like that. So I've learned to bring my thumb around the front of the harp, which allows me to create a large enough chamber to generate a good wah-wah effect. Experiment with both methods and see which works best for you.

Photo courtesy of Hohner

Big Walter Horton

FANNING

Now let's take a look at the technique of **fanning**. This is a more subtle technique than the wah, but it's still very expressive. The motion is similar to that of fanning yourself off on a hot day. The idea is to fan the air in front of the harmonica with your right hand while playing a note (blown or drawn). This can be done quickly or slowly, and the distance you move your right hand can vary as well for different effects. On the DVD, I demonstrate quicker and slower fanning techniques.

WARBLES, TRILLS, AND FLUTTERS

Some other effects include warbles, trills, and flutters. Whereas the wah-wah and fanning effects produce variations in *tone*, these produce variations in *pitch*. The warble and trill are similar, so let's start with those.

To perform a **warble**, blow or draw a note with your right hand on the right edge of the harmonica. Now, while playing the note, wiggle the harmonica back and forth so that your mouth moves between two holes repeatedly. This is a classic harmonica move that you've heard over and over. On a C harp, try drawing on hole 2 to produce a G note. Now use your right hand to wiggle the harp back and forth so that your mouth moves between the drawn G on hole 2 and the drawn B on hole 3.

A **trill** is similar in technique to a warble, but it's usually a little faster. Try using the same wiggling motion on the C harp to move between a drawn D (hole 4) and a drawn F (hole 5).

In music, both warbles and trills are indicated with a stemless note in parentheses following a rhythmic note. The above trill, for example, would be notated as such:

Sometimes the notes are more distinct, and sometimes they bleed together a bit more and sound like a dyad (a two-note chord). The former is accomplished with a more pronounced wiggling motion. Try experimenting with both methods, as they're both legitimate sounds that have their place.

A **flutter** is essentially the same principle (the rapid alternation of two notes), but it's performed with the tongue. You're blowing or drawing two (or three) holes at once, but the tongue is fluttering back and forth, alternately blocking each hole (or pair of holes). This is more difficult than the warble and trill and will take a bit of time to work up. Different players can accomplish this at different speeds, and you'll find that the tone is a bit different than the trill or warble. Try drawing holes 2–4 on your C harp and fluttering your tongue back and forth to match the effect on the DVD.

TONGUE ARTICULATION

To repeat the same note quickly, we can use the tongue to articulate the notes. This is done by maintaining a steady blow or draw while saying "ttt-ttt-ttt," "lah-de-lah," or another variant that involves the tongue making contact with the teeth. Try different things to see what works for you.

Here's a phrase I play on the DVD using this technique. I'm playing cross harp on a C harmonica. Notice that we start with a pre-bend here and release it as a way to create the illusion of an upward bend on a harmonica.

On the DVD, I demonstrate this idea in fast and slow tempos. Start off slowly, and once you can nail that, start moving toward the faster demo.

BASS NOTES

The bass notes on the harmonica are normally used to keep rhythm and percussive beats, as well as playing bass lines. This is especially useful when you're playing solo harp. You can really get people moving with these ideas.

Percussive Beats

Let's start with a basic rhythmic pattern on a C harp, playing cross harp in the key of G.

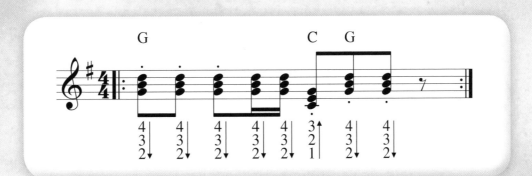

I'm using my tongue here for the articulation of the notes. Notice the small dots over the G chords. This is a **staccato** marking, and it means to play the notes short and abruptly. Until the blown C chord, the first several G chords are produced with one long, continuous inhale of breath. The tongue is used to articulate the rhythm. Say "ttt, ttt, ttt, ttt-ttt" (or something else if it's more comfortable for you) to create the rhythm.

When combining different tongue articulations with different cupped-hand effects, you can get quite a wide palette of sounds. Check out the DVD for a demonstration of this.

Or you can flutter the tongue up and down for even more unique sounds. Check out the DVD demonstration to hear how this sounds as well.

Bass Lines

Now let's check out some bass lines on the C harp. This first line begins with a first-hole blow and is played **straight harp** (i.e., in the key of the harp). We're using a whole-step bend on hole 3 to play the A note.

Now let's look at how we can do that playing cross harp. So we'll begin with a second-hole draw and play in the key of G on a C harp. We don't need to use any bends here.

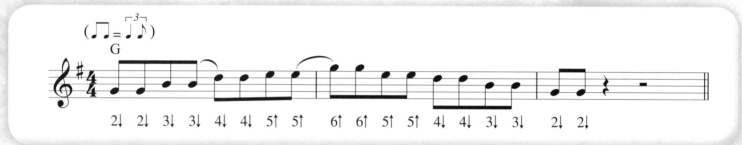

And here's a variation on the cross harp bass line in G; again, no bends are necessary.

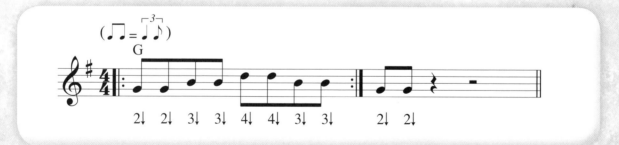

Work on becoming familiar with all of these and then try stringing them together. Play the G bass lines followed by the C or vice versa. They'll serve as the I (C) and V (G) chords in a C blues or as the I (G) and IV (C) chords in a G blues.

Jimmy Reed

POSITIONS AND KEYS

We can play in several different "positions" on a diatonic harp, which allows us to play in several different keys using one harp. Not only is this convenient, but it's also a requirement if you want to get certain licks or riffs. (Not all phrases are possible in every position/key.) You'll eventually develop your own repertoire of licks and riffs in each position, and you'll need to quickly be able to figure out the key/position transposition in order to play in the same key as the band. That's what this chapter is for.

FIRST POSITION (STRAIGHT HARP)

First position is the most obvious of all. You simply play in the key of the harp. This is sometimes called playing **straight harp**. If the harp says "A" on it, you're playing in the key of A. For simplicity's sake, all the positions discussed here will be in reference to an A diatonic harp. Your lower root notes are blow 1 and blow 4. **Transposition**: none.

Sample Phrase

This sample phrase is the last two measures of the example played on the DVD.

SECOND POSITION (CROSS HARP)

Playing in second position is known as **cross harp**. We've touched on this a bit already. On an A harmonica, this means playing in the key of the A major scale's fifth note: E. This is the most commonly used position for playing blues harp because it lays a bit more naturally. You just have to get used to the fact that you're drawing for the I chord (E)—not blowing! Your lower root notes are draw 2 (or blow 3) and blow 6. **Transposition**: up a perfect 5th from the key of the harp.

Sample Phrase

This sample phrase is the 17th and 18th measures of the example played on the DVD.

THIRD POSITION

In third position on an A harp, we're playing in the key of B. You can think of this as playing in the key of the A major scale's second note. This is probably the most common of all the upper positions (those above first and second position). Your lower root notes are draw 1 and draw 4. **Transposition**: up a major 2nd from the key of the harp.

Sample Phrase

This sample phrase is the first three measures of the example played on the DVD.

FOURTH POSITION

Fourth position is a difficult one and is not often used. On an A harp, it involves playing in the key of the A major scale's sixth note: F♯. It's not my position of expertise, but I'll do my best to demonstrate it. The lowest naturally occurring F♯ note on the A harp is draw 6, but you can get a low F♯ by bending the G♯ on draw 3 down a whole step. **Transposition**: up a major 6th from the key of the harp.

Sample Phrase

This sample phrase is the 4th and 5th measure of the example played on the DVD. The small notes in this phrase are called **grace notes**. A grace note is an embellishing note in front of a target note—G♯ in this case. A grace note takes up no rhythmic time; in these instances, you just quickly slide from draw 6 to draw 7.

FIFTH POSITION

In fifth position, we're playing in the key of C♯ or D♭ on an A harp. This means we're playing in the key of the A major scale's third note. The lower root notes are blow 2 and blow 5. This one has a surprising amount of workable notes in it. **Transposition**: up a major 3rd from the key of the harp.

Sample Phrase

This sample phrase is the pickup notes and first measure of the example played on the DVD. **Pickup notes** are notes that begin before the first measure of the song.

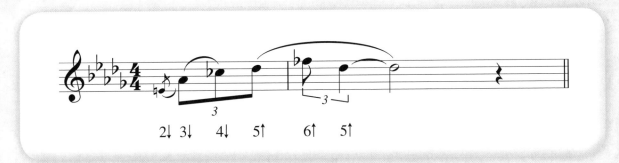

SIXTH POSITION

Sixth position involves playing in G♯ or A♭ with an A harp. In other words, we're playing in the key of the A major scale's seventh note. It's important to mention that this position is normally used to play in a minor key—in this case, G♯ minor. This means that we're mostly playing ♭3rds (three half steps above the tonic instead of four) and ♭7ths (a whole step below the tonic). You can hear this difference on the DVD. Think of a song like "The Thrill Is Gone," and you're hearing a minor blues. **Transposition**: down a minor 2nd from the key of the harp.

Sample Phrase

This sample phrase is the first two measures of the example played on the DVD.

USING MULTIPLE HARPS

In addition to playing in different positions on one harp, we can also do the same thing by using several harps in different keys. This allows access to different notes and riffs that aren't possible on one harp alone. This will take some getting used to, as the physical act of switching harps quickly takes some practice. But it really does open up a lot of possibilities. One word of caution: make sure you have your harps arranged so that you can quickly grab the right one in a dimly lit club. If you grab the wrong one by mistake, it could get ugly!

First and Second Position

One common method is to use one harp to play straight harp (first position) and another to play cross harp (second position). If you're playing a blues in the key of A, for example, you'd use an A harp (for straight harp) and a D harp (for cross harp).

Don't get confused by this! Earlier in this chapter when we talked about cross harp, we mentioned playing in the key of E on an A harp. This time, we'll be playing in the key of A, so we can't use an A harp for cross harp. Our transposition rule says *up a perfect 5th from the key of the harp*. Another way to say this, when you know the key of the blues but not the harp, is *down a 5th from the key of the blues*. So in this case we can count down five notes of the A major scale:

A (1) – G♯ (2) – F♯ (3) – E (4) – D (5)

Therefore, we need a D-tuned harmonica to play cross harp in the key of A. So check out the DVD to hear a demonstration of me switching between A and D harps over an A blues.

First, Second, and Third Position

You can also switch between three harps to get even more sounds. In this example, we'll still play a blues in A, but I'll add a G harp to the A and D harps from the previous example. On the G harp, I'll be playing third position (a major 2nd up from the key of the harp). This can get confusing, so you have to maintain your concentration!

Third Position and Chromatic

Another method, popularized by the late, great Little Walter, is to switch between third position on a diatonic harp and a chromatic harp. In the key of D, for example, this would mean using a C diatonic and a C chromatic. Little Walter did just this for the classic recording of Muddy Waters' "I Just Want to Make Love to You." This is widely acknowledged as the first use of chromatic harp in the blues world. Check out the DVD to hear an example of this.

PENTATONIC SCALES

If you want to play a blues solo on the harp, you need to know which notes to use, and that's where scales come in. A **scale** is simply a collection of notes that we use to build phrases and chords. When you hear someone playing a solo (on any instrument), they're working with the notes of a scale (or sometimes several scales) to create melodies.

We've already learned a few ways to play the C major scale on a diatonic C harp. And though we haven't actually demonstrated it, these major scale patterns would transfer to the key of any diatonic harp. In other words, if you played the same pattern of 4↑ 4↓ 5↑ 5↓ 6↑ 6↓ 7↓ 7↑ on a D-tuned harp, you'd have a D major scale. If you play it on an A-tune harp, you'd have an A major scale, etc. In fact, it should be stated (in case it's not obvious) that any lick, riff, or phrase we play on one diatonic harp can usually be played on any diatonic harp; it will just be transposed to the key of the new harp. (I say "can usually" be played because there are some bends that are more difficult on certain harps. However, we won't be playing anything like that in this book.)

Though the major scale is an incredibly useful scale, it's not used all that much in blues soloing. More often, **pentatonic** scales are used to play blues licks. They're called pentatonic because they contain five different notes, as opposed to a major scale, which contains seven different notes. (You may look back up at the pattern shown above and count eight notes. But there are actually only seven *different* notes; the top one, 7↑, is the same note as the bottom one, 4↑, only an octave higher.)

By using only five notes, pentatonic scales get rid of some of the notes that sound a bit out of place if not used correctly. In other words, pentatonic scales contain mostly all "safe" notes. There are two different types of pentatonic scales we'll cover here: the **major pentatonic scale** and the **minor pentatonic scale**.

MAJOR PENTATONIC SCALE

If we think of the major scale's "formula" as 1–2–3–4–5–6–7, where each number represents a degree of the scale, then we have a reference point for creating formulas of other scales. The formula for a major pentatonic scale, for example, is simply 1–2–3–5–6. So you can see that it's the same as the major scale, but the fourth and seventh tones have been omitted.

A C major pentatonic scale would therefore contain the notes C–D–E–G–A. We can play this scale all the way up and down the harp, and only one bend is required. Here's how it looks on a C harp.

C Major Pentatonic Scale on C-Tuned Harmonica

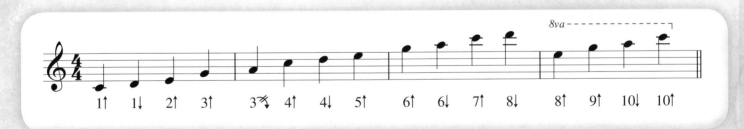

In a C blues, this would fit the I (tonic) chord (C or C7) nicely. It would also work fairly well over the V (dominant) chord (G or G7).

F Major Pentatonic Scale on C-Tuned Harmonica

We can also play an F major pentatonic scale (F–G–A–C–D) on a C harp with relative ease. This would fit the IV (subdominant) chord (F or F7). Notice that it requires two bends on the lower end, but the upper ranges can be played without bends.

G Major Pentatonic Scale on C-Tuned Harmonica

We can play the G major pentatonic scale (G–A–B–D–E) on a C harp as well. This would fit the V (dominant) chord (G or G7). This will require only one bend in the lower register.

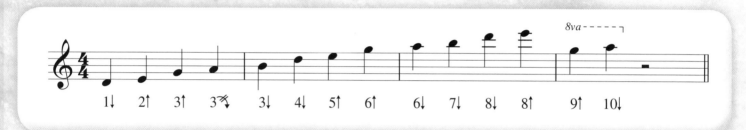

Major Pentatonic Scale Summary – Blues in C

So let's look at which major pentatonic scales will work over which chords in a 12-bar blues. We'll use a C blues here, but these concepts can be transposed to any harp for any blues key.

- **Over I (tonic) chord (C or C7)**: C major pentatonic
- **Over IV (subdominant) chord (F or F7)**: F major pentatonic
- **Over V (dominant) chord (G or G7)**: G major pentatonic or C major pentatonic

MINOR PENTATONIC SCALE

The minor pentatonic scale is even more common in the blues than the major pentatonic. Whereas the major pentatonic sounds cheerful and more country-flavored, the minor pentatonic will sound tougher and bluesier. The formula for a minor pentatonic scale is 1–♭3–4–5–♭7. This is just like a C minor scale with the second and sixth tones removed. We haven't looked at a C minor scale yet, so here it is:

C–D–E♭–F–G–A♭–B♭

So, if we remove the 2nd (D) and 6th (A♭), we'll end up with the C minor pentatonic scale:

C–E♭–F–G–B♭

However, we could still reach these notes by following the formula as it relates to the major scale. Our minor pentatonic formula is 1–♭3–4–5–♭7, so we start with the first, third, fourth, fifth, and seventh notes of the C major scale:

C–E–F–G–B

Now we lower the third and seventh notes by a half step (indicated by ♭), and we end up with the same C minor pentatonic scale:

C–E♭–F–G–B♭

Now here's where it gets a bit tricky. We can't really play a C minor pentatonic scale very well on a C harp. We can get some of the notes easily, like C, F, G, and B♭. But the only really solid E♭ we can get is on the eighth-hole blow by bending down a half step.

This is another reason that playing cross harp is so common in the blues. If we played cross harp on a C harp, we'd be playing in the key of G. The I, IV, and V chords in a G blues are G (or G7), C (or C7), and D (or D7). Whereas with the major pentatonic scale, we could use each chord's respective major pentatonic scale (C major pentatonic over C, F major pentatonic over F, etc.), the minor pentatonic doesn't work quite that way.

We can use the respective minor pentatonic scale over the I and V chords well. In the key of G, this would mean playing G minor pentatonic over G (I) and D minor pentatonic over D (V). But you'll find if you use the IV chord's respective minor pentatonic scale (C minor pentatonic over C, in this case), it tends to sound pretty sour.

So let's take a step back and get some clarity. We were talking about a blues in C, and now we're talking about a blues in G. So what's going on? Basically, if you want to solo with major pentatonic scales exclusively, you can play straight harp and you'll do fine. Again, this means playing a C harp over a C blues. This will tend to sound brighter and more like country blues.

However, if you want to play the grittier stuff and use minor pentatonics, then you'll want to play cross harp. With a C harp, this means playing over a G blues. We've already covered the straight harp approach, so let's discuss the cross harp approach now.

G Minor Pentatonic Scale on C-Tuned Harmonica

Here's how the G minor pentatonic scale (G–B♭–C–D–F) lays out on the C harp. This works well over all three chords of a G blues: G or G7 (I), C or C7 (IV), and D or D7 (V). As you can see, we can't get all the notes all the way up, but we can get most of them.

We've already mentioned that playing C minor pentatonic in a G blues isn't common at all, so we won't bother with that.

D Minor Pentatonic Scale on C-Tuned Harmonica

And here's the D minor pentatonic scale (D–F–G–A–C) on the C harp. This works well over the V chord (D or D7), but is occasionally used over the I chord (G or G7) briefly for a different sound. It actually shares a lot of notes with the G minor pentatonic scale; only one note is different.

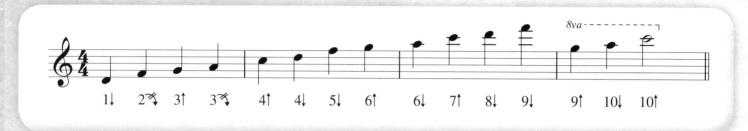

Minor Pentatonic Scale Summary – Blues in G

So let's look at which minor pentatonic scales will work over which chords in a 12-bar blues. We'll use a G blues here, but these concepts can be transposed to any harp (playing cross harp) for any blues key.

- **Over I (tonic) chord (G or G7)**: G minor pentatonic or D minor pentatonic
- **Over IV (subdominant) chord (C or C7)**: G minor pentatonic
- **Over V (dominant) chord (D or D7)**: D minor pentatonic or G minor pentatonic

Remember, we've talked about several different chords and scales here, but the one constant has been the C harp. We've been playing all these scales on a C harp. Now let's take a look at the possibilities available when we combine major and minor pentatonic scales in a G blues.

COMBINED MAJOR AND MINOR PENTATONIC SCALE SUMMARY – BLUES IN G

- **Over I (tonic) chord (G or G7)**: G minor pentatonic, G major pentatonic, or D minor pentatonic
- **Over IV (subdominant) chord (C or C7)**: C major pentatonic or G minor pentatonic
- **Over V (dominant) chord (D or D7)**: D minor pentatonic, G minor pentatonic, or G major pentatonic

Sample Licks

When I say "you can play X scale over X chord," I don't mean you just play the scale up and down. I mean you use the notes of the scale to come up with melodies, or **licks**. Here we'll take a look at a few sample licks using some of the scales we covered. These will all be played on a C harp. Practice the scales shown in this chapter. Once you have them down, come back here to try your hand at these licks.

Lick 1: G Minor Pentatonic

In beat 2 of this lick, we begin with draw 4 pre-bent down a half step to C♯ and then quickly let it return to its unbent D note.

Lick 2: G Minor Pentatonic

Lick 3: G Major Pentatonic

Lick 4: G Major Pentatonic

Lick 5: C Major Pentatonic

Lick 6: D Minor Pentatonic

CLASSIC BLUES RIFFS

Now that you've got a good amount of material under your belt, let's put it to use and learn some classic blues harp riffs. Many of these will be instantly recognizable to you, and they'll add instant legitimacy to your harp playing. These types of things work great at open mics and informal settings, often times inspiring a full-fledged jam. Take your time working these up, but have fun in the process. This is what blues harp is all about!

We'll play all of these on a C harp, and I'll not only indicate the key, but also if they're played straight harp, cross harp, or in another position.

RIFF 1, KEY OF G (CROSS HARP)

This is one of the most classic harp licks of all time. There are a lot of variations on it, but here's a basic version that will serve you well. Inspired by songs like "Mannish Boy" and "Hoochie Coochie Man" (both by Muddy Waters) or "I'm a Man" by Bo Diddley, this riff is sure to get some feet stompin' and heads bobbin'.

RIFF 2, KEY OF G (CROSS HARP)

Here's a classic boogie-style bass line riff that's played cross harp style with no bends necessary. This is a great one to play when you're by yourself, as it will get people tapping their feet for sure. Remember, when playing several draw notes in a row like this, use your tongue to articulate the notes. If you were to try to take individual breaths for each of these notes, you'd run out of air quickly. The first three beats of this riff should be played with one continuous draw; use the tongue to separate the notes.

Junior Wells

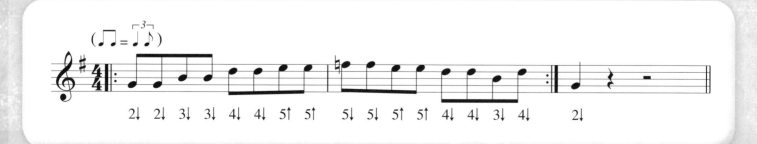

RIFF 3, KEY OF G (CROSS HARP)

This is a classic ending phrase that you can play at the end of a 12-bar blues. You'd give the cue to the band in measure 10, and this lick would start at measure 11. The band will accent the last three notes with you. Notice the octaves at the beginning.

James Cotton

Paul Butterfield

RIFF 4, KEY OF G (CROSS HARP)

This one makes a good intro to a blues, or you can use it in a solo as well. The hardest part will be getting the half-step pre-bend on the fourth hole, so really make sure you're getting that before speeding it up.

RIFF 5, KEY OF C (STRAIGHT HARP)

Here's a classic major pentatonic riff in C played straight harp on a C harp. This one is another good intro and works well in slow or fast tempos. You can repeat this one to build some momentum too.

4↑ 5↑ 6↑ 6↓ 7↑   4↑ 5↑ 6↑ 6↓ 7↑

Sonny Terry

Slim Harpo

RIFF 6, KEY OF G (CROSS HARP)

This one makes a nice variation to Riff 1.

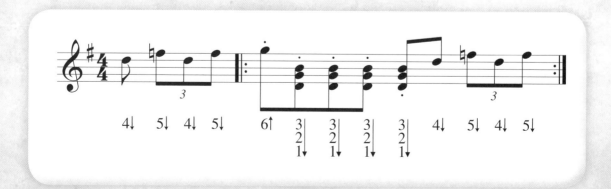

4↓ 5↓ 4↓ 5↓   6↑ 3/2/1↓ 3/2/1↓ 3/2/1↓ 3/2/1↓ 4↓ 5↓ 4↓ 5↓

PLAYING IN A BAND

Although you can have plenty of fun playing the harp all by your lonesome, it's a heck of a lot of fun playing with a band as well. If you're just jamming with some acoustic instruments, you won't need any other equipment, but if you're going to hit the stage, you'll need to amplify your harp so you can be heard. In this chapter, we're going to look at what that entails, and how it changes the tone of your harp.

ACOUSTIC VS. ELECTRIC

As mentioned, if you're playing with acoustic instruments or very soft electric instruments, an unamplified (a.k.a. "acoustic") harp will work fine. The range of the harp is such that it's well suited to be a lead instrument, so it's not too tough to project above soft pianos, guitars, etc. Listen to the DVD to hear an example of me playing unamplified along with soft electric guitar accompaniment.

If you're playing with a fully rocking band, or if you just want a different tone, you can either play your harp into a vocal microphone that's plugged into a P.A. or play into a specially designed microphone that's plugged into a harp amp. The latter is the preferred method for blues harp, as the distortion generated from the amp is desirable. (We'll talk more about gear specifics in the Appendix.) Now check out the DVD to hear the difference in sound when I play with a mic through an amp.

DIFFERENT BAND FORMATS

Your role as a harp player will change slightly depending on the size and type of ensemble. Knowing the chord changes is not enough; you also need to know when to play and when not to play. So let's examine some of the modifications you may make when performing in each.

Playing in a Duo

It's very common for a harp player to play in a duo setting, so let's start there. This is most often with a guitar player, but it could also be with a pianist or even a bassist. In this format, you'll be filling up a good amount of space with the harp, adding chords and perhaps some bass lines to help lend support to the other instrument. Listen to the DVD for an example of this.

Playing in a duo

Playing in a Trio or Quartet

When adding a third instrument, such as a piano or bass, your playing will change noticeably from the duo style. You'll have two other instruments to listen to, and the chance of clashing with or stepping on the feet of one of them is that much greater. Being conscious of the other player's tendencies, sounds, and feel is critical to achieving a good blend. This will come with experience and practice; you'll probably end up making a few mistakes in this regard, but as long as you learn from them, they're worth it!

In a quartet, you'll most likely be playing with a drummer, which will bring about the biggest change in your playing. If you're playing with a drummer, it means that everything else will be louder to compete with the volume of the drums. This makes amplified harp a likely necessity, and it means you'll really have to feel out your role in the ensemble. You'll usually play much less than with a duo, with the obvious exception of your solo spot—should you get one. It's also quite possible that, if you're playing with a quartet, one of the other members will be singing as well. And audiences really don't like when they're not able to hear the vocals! This brings us to our next point…

Backing Up a Vocalist

Whether you're playing in a duo, trio, or quartet format, when there's a singer, the game changes dramatically. The number one focus is the vocal (at least from the audience's standpoint), and therefore you **do not** want to step on his or her toes. This means that you'll either be adding brief fills in between vocal phrases or possibly laying out altogether for a whole verse if another instrument is providing the fills. Another possibility is sustaining soft chords at parts of the verse. Percussive rhythms, however, will usually draw too much attention and should normally be avoided.

The vocal line in the blues normally follows a set pattern and cadence that can usually be determined before even the first verse is through. Once you're sure of this pattern, you can start adding support by filling in the dead spots between vocal lines. Again, make sure you're not stepping on the toes of another player who has the same thing in mind. If there is more than one solo instrument in the band, it's common to alternate fills from verse to verse.

Check out the DVD to hear me accompanying Billy as he plays guitar and sings. Notice that I get in and out quickly between his vocal phrases—sometimes playing literally only one or two notes. You'd be surprised by how much this adds to the sound. Even those one- or two-note fills are important.

Photo by Bob Pierce

Playing in a quartet

PLAYING BEHIND OR AHEAD OF THE BEAT

When playing by yourself, you're supplying all the rhythm; in essence, you are "the beat." But when you're playing in a band, there will be a rhythm section—often bass, drums, and either piano or guitar (or both)—and they'll maintain the beat on their own. This means that you can choose where to place your notes with reference to that established beat.

By playing slightly behind or ahead of that beat, you can generate different emotions or moods than when playing strictly in time. On the DVD I demonstrate this by filling in between my own vocals accompanied by Billy on guitar. Listen to how I'm fluctuating between playing behind the beat to on the beat to slightly ahead of the beat at times and notice the effect it has.

LEAVING SPACE

There's no need to hurry in music. When you're starting out, you may feel the need to fill up every possible moment with every lick you know. This can be impressive at times, but often it's the player that says only what needs to be said with very little that makes the biggest impact. Of course the flashy playing can be fun, and I'm not saying it has no merit. All I'm saying is that patience and restraint can make a powerful statement too, and you should definitely experiment with it to help broaden your horizons as a player.

This obviously applies not only to solo playing, but also during vocal verses or while backing up other solos as well, as I've already mentioned. As an exercise, try singing a solo and then mimicking what you sing. This can be valuable even if you can't carry a tune; the emphasis here is on phrasing, which largely has to do with rhythm. And everyone can sing in rhythm, if not in tune. On the DVD, I illustrate how leaving space sounds.

Call and Response

While on the subject of leaving space, we should address the idea of **call and response**, as the two often go hand in hand. The idea is that you trade off lead responsibilities with another band member. This could be a guitar player, pianist, or even the singer. You play one phrase, they play the next. And back and forth you go. It's a lot of fun for both the musicians and the audience. Check it out on the DVD.

DYNAMICS, ACCENTS, AND PHRASING

The blues is all about feeling, and the more you put into it, the better it sounds. Check out the several examples on the DVD that demonstrate the use of playing with **dynamics** (varying the volume of your phrases) and **accents** (adding stress to certain notes), and listen to the points I make about **phrasing**.

CONCLUSION

I hope the information I've provided here will help you become a better player. Utilizing these concepts will guide you in discovering different ways to play the blues—both in soloing and accompanying others. Remember that Rome wasn't built in a day; many of the techniques covered in this book will take time to develop. Don't get discouraged if something is particularly difficult for you. Stick with it, practice regularly (daily if possible), and the results will come. Blues harmonica is an incredibly rewarding instrument, and I wish you all the best in your pursuit.

-Steve Guyger

RECOMMENDED LISTENING

Here's a list of some harmonica albums, in no particular order, that I definitely recommend checking out. Each one is rife with top-notch harp playing.

- *Harmonica Ace* (Little George Smith)
- *I Couldn't Believe My Eyes* (Sonny Terry)
- *Sonny's Story* (Sonny Terry)
- *At Newport* (Muddy Waters – featuring James Cotton on harp)
- *The Definitive Collection* (Muddy Waters – featuring Little Walter Jacobs on harp)
- *Hate to See You Go* (Little Walter Jacobs)
- *Little Boy Blue* (Big Walter Horton)
- *Blue Bird Blues* (John Lee "Sonny Boy" Williamson)
- *Down and Out Blues* (Rice Miller, a.k.a. "Sonny Boy Williamson")
- *Hoodoo Man Blues* (Junior Wells)
- *High Compression* (James Cotton)
- *The Chess Box* (Howlin' Wolf)
- *The Paul Butterfield Blues Band* (Paul Butterfield)

Paul Butterfield

Howlin' Wolf

This list is by no means comprehensive, but it's a great place to start. Enjoy digging deep and discovering other great harp albums. The search is half the fun!

APPENDIX

CHARTS FOR BACKING TRACKS

At the end of the DVD, there are several backing tracks for you to practice with. They're all in the key of E, so you'll use an E-tuned harmonica to play straight harp and an A-tuned for cross harp. Here are the charts for those tracks.

12-Bar Blues in E

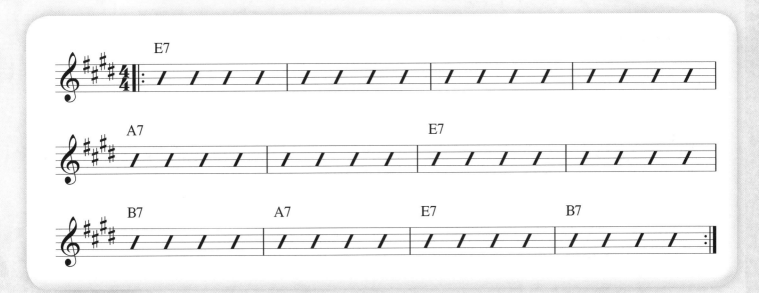

12-Bar Blues with Quick Change in E

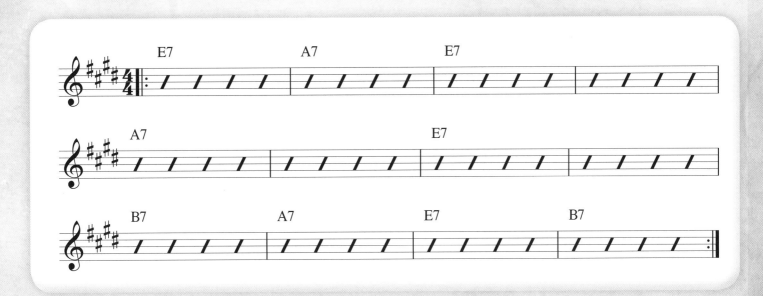

8-Bar Blues in E

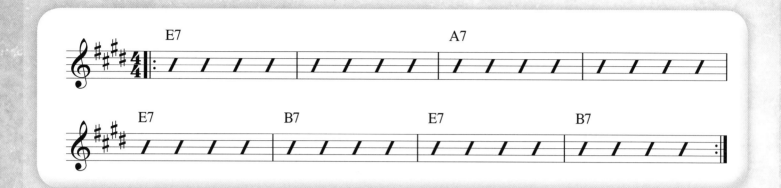

I-Chord Blues in E

A BRIEF CHORD THEORY PRIMER

Chords are built from intervals, or degrees, of notes from a major (or minor) scale. A major scale contains seven notes, and those notes are numbered 1 through 7. (The 1 is also commonly referred to as the "root" or "tonic.") So if a chord contains the root, 3rd, and 5th, then it contains the 1st, 3rd, and 5th notes of the root's major scale. If it contains a root, ♭3rd, and 5th, then the 3rd is lowered by a half step. This is referred to as a chord's **formula**.

In order to understand how the chords in this book are built, you simply need to know all twelve major scales, which are shown in this Appendix, and apply the formula to a particular root note.

For example, the formula for a major chord is root, 3rd, 5th (or 1–3–5). If you want to understand how a C major chord is built, you would look in the Appendix to find the C major scale. Its notes are C–D–E–F–G–A–B (no sharps or flats). Take the 1st (C), 3rd (E), and 5th (G) notes, and you have the chord. So, a C major chord is spelled C–E–G.

In this book, we only deal with major chords (such as G, for example) and dominant seventh chords (such as G7). The only difference between a major chord and a seventh chord is the presence of the ♭7th in the seventh chord. So a dominant seventh chord's formula is 1–3–5–♭7. To build a G7 chord, you would first look at the notes of a G major scale: G–A–B–C–D–E–F♯. Then you would take the 1st, 3rd, 5th, and 7th: G–B–D–F♯. Since we need a ♭7th, we lower the 7th down a half step from F♯ to F. So a G7 chord is spelled G–B–D–F.

You can use these formulas, along with the following list of major scales, to spell any chord mentioned in this book. Remember, almost all blues consists of the I, IV, and V chords in any key. Just find the first, fourth, and fifth notes of any major scale, and you have your roots for those I, IV, and V chords, respectively.

Twelve Major Scales

C major: C–D–E–F–G–A–B

G major: G–A–B–C–D–E–F♯

D major: D–E–F♯–G–A–B–C♯

A major: A–B–C♯–D–E–F♯–G♯

E major: E–F♯–G♯–A–B–C♯–D♯

B major: B–C♯–D♯–E–F♯–G♯–A♯

F major: F–G–A–B♭–C–D–E

B♭ major: B♭–C–D–E♭–F–G–A

E♭ major: E♭–F–G–A♭–B♭–C–D

A♭ major: A♭–B♭–C–D♭–E♭–F–G

D♭ major: D♭–E♭–F–G♭–A♭–B♭–C

G♭ major: G♭–A♭–B♭–C♭–D♭–E♭–F

EQUIPMENT

Harmonicas

It goes without saying that if you want to be prepared to play a blues in any key, you should own a harp in every key. This can get pricey if you're on a tight budget—especially if you're buying quality harps—so determine what kind of ensemble you'll be playing with first, as that will let you know which harps to buy first. If you'll be playing mostly with guitarists, you need the sharp key harps. I'd suggest A first, so you can play cross harp in the key of E, which is probably the most common blues key for guitar. Then, you can acquire D, C, and G harps and add from there.

Harps don't last forever. Their lifespan will vary greatly depending on how often and how hard you play them, but typically you'll need to replace them between every three or four months (if played regularly) to every year or so (with lighter use). Usually, they will first lose their ability to play in tune very well. Eventually, metal fatigue will set in, and the harp will often produce no sound at all through certain holes. To prolong the life of your harps, try to not play any harder than necessary, keep it in its case when not in use, and avoid getting it wet (which leads to rust). Remember to tap it on your leg each time you finish playing it to help get rid of any excess moisture.

Microphones

The mic of choice for the Chicago blues harmonica player is the **bullet mic**. They were cheap and affordable back in the day, and therefore their tone became intertwined with the music they helped produce. The bullet mic produces the classic dirty, distorted tone that's so commonplace in Chicago blues. There are many on the market today by brands like Shure, so if you don't want to shell out the bucks for an authentic vintage one, you have plenty of options. Typically, a bullet mic will come with an attached cable with a 1/4" plug at the end, which is perfect for plugging into an amp.

Shure 520DX bullet microphone

In a pinch, you can get by with a vocal dynamic mic, such as a Shure SM58 or SM57. These are cheaper than the bullet mics, but the sound is much cleaner and therefore won't give you that typical blues dirt. But that's not the only difference. The bullet mic happens to be shaped very much like a cupped hand, which is another reason why it's so common. A dynamic vocal mic will be a bit more unwieldy in this regard.

Shure SM58 dynamic microphone

Amplifiers

At the other end of the mic cord must be some kind of amp. One possibility is to just plug the mic straight into the P.A.—the same way vocals are amplified. This will make you loud enough, but you'll have the least amount of flexibility with your tone. It'll work in a pinch, but it won't get that authentic Chicago tone. To get that classic Chicago blues harp sound, you'll most likely want to plug into a tube amp.

There are many different options in this regard, but low-wattage guitar amps are a popular choice. The tweed Fender Champ (5 watts), Kalamazoo Model Two (10 watts), Victoria 518-T (a replica of the tweed Fender Champ), Vox AC-4, and Kendrick Texas Crude Harp Amp are all tried and true tone machines. These can run anywhere from $1,000 (for a vintage tweed Fender Champ in good condition) to sometimes under $100 (for some Kalamazoo amps).

Tweed Fender Champ

Kalamazoo Model Two

Vox AC-4

What's great about these low-wattage amps is that they don't get terribly loud, yet they begin to distort at relatively low volumes. Most of the time, unless you're playing a very small club, the soundman will mic the amp and run that through the P.A.—the same method usually employed for the guitar amps. So don't be under the impression that your amp needs to be loud enough to fill a huge venue; that's not the way it works. In all but the smallest venues, the amps are always miked and run through the P.A. The difference is that, instead of blasting your clean, unaffected harp through the P.A.—as is the case when you just play into a dynamic vocal mic—you're blasting your warm, fuzzy, distorted harp through the P.A. How sweet it sounds!

HARMONICA NOTATION LEGEND

Harmonica music can be notated two different ways: on a *musical staff*, and in *tablature*.

THE MUSICAL STAFF shows pitches and rhythms and is divided by bar lines into measures. Pitches are named after the first seven letters of the alphabet.

TABLATURE graphically represents the harmonica music. Each note will be accompanied by a number, 1 through 10, indicating what hole you are to play. The arrow that follows indicates whether to blow or draw. (All examples are shown using a C diatonic harmonica.)

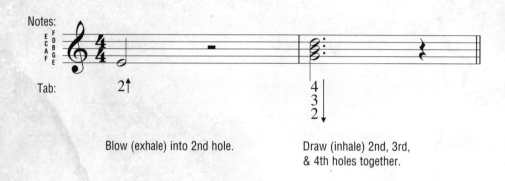

Blow (exhale) into 2nd hole.

Draw (inhale) 2nd, 3rd, & 4th holes together.

Notes on the C Harmonica

Exhaled (Blown) Notes

1 2 3 4 5 6 7 8 9 10

C E G C E G C E G C

Inhaled (Drawn) Notes

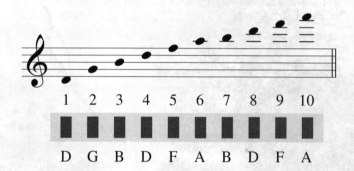

1 2 3 4 5 6 7 8 9 10

D G B D F A B D F A

Bends

Blow Bends

- 1/4 step
- 1/2 step
- 1 step
- 1 1/2 steps

Draw Bends

- 1/4 step
- 1/2 step
- 1 step
- 1 1/2 steps

Definitions for Special Harmonica Notation

SLURRED BEND: Play (draw) 3rd hole, then bend the note down one whole step.

GRACE NOTE BEND: Starting with a pre-bent note, immediately release bend to the target note.

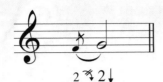

VIBRATO: Begin adding vibrato to the sustained note on beat 3.

TONGUE BLOCKING: Using your tongue to block holes 2 & 3, play octaves on holes 1 & 4.

TRILL: Shake the harmonica rapidly to alternate between notes.

NOTE: Tablature numbers in parentheses are used when:

- The note is sustained, but a new articulation begins (such as vibrato), or
- The quantity of notes being sustained changes, or
- A change in dynamics (volume) occurs.
- It's the alternate note in a trill.

Additional Musical Definitions

D.S. al Coda — • Go back to the sign (𝄋), then play until the measure marked *"To Coda,"* then skip to the section labelled *"Coda."*

D.C. al Fine — • Go back to the beginning of the song and play until the measure marked *"Fine"* (end).

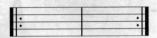 • Repeat measures between signs.

 *(accent)* • Accentuate the note (play initial attack louder).

(staccato) • Play the note short.

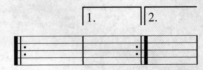 • When a repeated section has different endings, play the first ending only the first time and the second ending only the second time.

Dynamics

p • Piano (soft)

mp • Mezzo Piano (medium soft)

mf • Mezzo Forte (medium loud)

f • Forte (loud)

(crescendo) • Gradually louder

(decrescendo) • Gradually softer

The Harmonica Play-Along Series
Play your favorite songs quickly and easily!

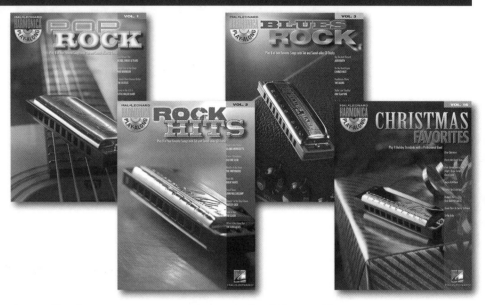

Just follow the notation, listen to the CD to hear how the harmonica should sound, and then play along using the separate full-band backing tracks. The melody and lyrics are also included in the book in case you want to sing, or to simply help you follow along. The audio CD is playable on any CD player. For PC and MAC computer users, the CD is enhanced so you can adjust the recording to any tempo without changing pitch!

1. Pop/Rock
And When I Die • Bright Side of the Road • I Should Have Known Better • Low Rider • Miss You • Piano Man • Take the Long Way Home • You Don't Know How It Feels.
00000478...$14.99

2. Rock Hits
Cowboy • Hand in My Pocket • Karma Chameleon • Middle of the Road • Run Around • Smokin' in the Boys Room • Train in Vain • What I like About You.
00000479...$14.99

3. Blues/Rock
Big Ten Inch Record • On the Road Again • Roadhouse Blues • Rollin' and Tumblin' • Train Kept A-Rollin' • Train, Train • Waitin' for the Bus • You Shook Me.
00000481...$14.99

4. Folk/Rock
Blowin' in the Wind • Catch the Wind • Daydream • Eve of Destruction • Me and Bobby McGee • Mr. Tambourine Man • Pastures of Plenty.
00000482...$14.99

5. Country Classics
Blue Bayou • Don't Tell Me Your Troubles • He Stopped Loving Her Today • Honky Tonk Blues • If You've Got the Money (I've Got the Time) • The Only Daddy That Will Walk the Line • Orange Blossom Special • Whiskey River.
00001004...$14.99

6. Country Hits
Ain't Goin' down ('Til the Sun Comes Up) • Drive (For Daddy Gene) • Getcha Some • Here's a Quarter (Call Someone Who Cares) • Honkytonk U • One More Last Chance • Put Yourself in My Shoes • Turn It Loose.
00001013...$14.99

9. Chicago Blues
Blues with a Feeling • Easy • Got My Mo Jo Working • Help Me • I Ain't Got You • Juke • Messin' with the Kid.
00001091...$14.99

10. Blues Classics
Baby, Scratch My Back • Eyesight to the Blind • Good Morning Little Schoolgirl • Honest I Do • I'm Your Hoochie Coochie Man • My Babe • Ride and Roll • Sweet Home Chicago.
00001093...$14.99

11. Christmas Carols
Angels We Have Heard on High • Away in a Manger • Deck the Hall • The First Noel • Go, Tell It on the Mountain • Jingle Bells • Joy to the World • O Little Town of Bethlehem.
00001296...$12.99

13. Little Walter
Can't Hold Out Much Longer • Crazy Legs • I Got to Go • Last Night • Mean Old World • Rocker • Sad Hours • You're So Fine.
00001334...$14.99

15. Jazz Classics
All Blues • Au Privave • Comin' Home Baby • Song for My Father • Sugar • Sunny • Take Five • Work Song.
00001336 ....$14.99

16. Christmas Favorites
Blue Christmas • Frosty the Snow Man • Here Comes Santa Claus (Right down Santa Claus Lane) • Jingle-Bell Rock • Nuttin' for Christmas • Rudolph the Red-Nosed Reindeer • Santa Claus Is Comin' to Town • Silver Bells.
00001350...$14.99